# Carmichael Surname

# Ireland: 1600s to 1900s

From Ireland Church Records of Baptism, Marriage and Death

Comprised of Roman Catholic and Church of Ireland Records

From Counties Carlow, Cork, Kerry and Dublin City

Compiled by **Donovan Hurst**

January 15, 2013

# Dedication

This work is dedicated to all of those that came before us and shaped our lives to make us the people that we are today.

# Table of Contents

# Introduction

This is a compilation of individuals who have the surname of Carmichael that lived in the country of Ireland from the 1600s to the 1900s. I have placed each entry into one of four categories: Families, Individual Births/Baptisms, Individual Burials, and Individual Marriages. If a marriage entry primarily concerns an Individual Carmichael whom is female, then I have placed that entry under the category of Individual Marriages. If a marriage entry primarily concerns an Individual Carmichael whom is male, then I have placed that entry under the category of Families. Images of many of these listings are available at http://churchrecords.irishgenealogy.ie/churchrecords/.

To help guide the reader of this work, the format of this book is as follows:

- Main Family Entry (Husband and Wife) (Father and Mother)

  o Child of Main Family Entry, including Spouse(s) when available

    ▪ Grandchild of Main Family Entry, including Spouse(s) when available

      • Great-Grandchild of Main Family Entry, including Spouse(s) when available

(**Bolded Text**) following any entry includes any additional information such as Residence(s), Occupation(s), Signature(s), etc. when available.

# Hurst

Some of the fonts used in this work symbolizes Celtic writing.  The traditional letters, numbers, and punctuation marks and their Celtic counterparts are as follows:

Traditional Letters (Uppercase & Lowercase)

A a B b C c D d E f G g H h I i J j K k L l M m N n O o P p Q q R r S s T t U u V v W w X x Y y Z z

Celtic Letters (Uppercase & Lowercase)

A a B b C c D ð E e F ƒ G g H ƕ I í J j K k L l M m

N n O o P p Q q R ʀ S s T t U u V ʋ W ɯ X x Y ɣ Z z

Traditional Numbers

1 2 3 4 5 6 7 8 9 10

Celtic Numbers

1 2 3 4 5 6 7 8 9 10

Traditional Punctuation

. , : ' " & - ( )

Celtic Punctuation

. , : ' " & - ( )

# Parish Churches

# Carlow (Church of Ireland)

Carlow Parish.

# Cork & Ross
# (Roman Catholic or RC)

Cork - South Parish and Cork - SS. Peter & Paul Parish.

# Dublin (Church of Ireland)

Arbour Hill Barracks Parish, Clontarf Parish, Irishtown Parish, Molyneux Chapel Parish, St. Anne Parish, St. Audoen Parish, St. Barnabas Parish, St. Bride Parish, St. Catherine Parish, St. George Parish, St. James Parish, St. Luke Parish, St. Mark Parish, St. Mary Parish, St. Michael Parish, St. Michan Parish, St. Nicholas Without Parish, St. Paul Parish, St. Peter Parish, St. Thomas Parish, St. Werburgh Parish, and Taney Parish.

# Dublin (Roman Catholic or RC)

Clondalkin Parish, Harrington Street Parish, Rathmines Parish, Saggart Parish, SS. Michael & John Parish, St. Agatha Parish. St. Andrew Parish, St. Catherine Parish, St. James Parish, St. Mary, Pro Cathedral Parish, St. Michan Parish, and St. Nicholas Parish.

# Kerry (Church of Ireland)

Dromod & Prior Parish and Valentia Parish.

# Families

- Andrew Carmichael & Elizabeth Lloyd Roberts – 25 Oct 1827 (Marriage, **St. Peter Parish**)

**Andrew Carmichael (husband):**

Residence - Rutland Square - October 25, 1827

**Elizabeth Lloyd Roberts (wife):**

Residence - Harcourt Street - October 25, 1827

**Wedding Witnesses:**

**Martha Carmichael & Owen Roberts Quinn**

- Andrew Carmichael & Jane Caldbeck – 13 Sep 1801 (Marriage, **St. Mary Parish**)
- Andrew Blair Carmichael, b. 1775, bur. 9 Oct 1851 (Burial, **St. George Parish**) & Jane Swift, b. 1795, bur. 25 Nov 1864 (Burial, **St. George Parish**) – 15 Jul 1825 (Marriage, **St. Peter Parish**)
  - Arthur Frederick Carmichael – b. 7 Oct 1816, bapt. 15 Dec 1816 (Baptism, **St. Peter Parish**)
  - Hugh Carmichael – b. 4 Aug 1818, bapt. 11 Aug 1818 (Baptism, **St. Peter Parish**)
  - Jane Carmichael – b. 12 Sep 1826, bapt. 7 Nov 1826 (Baptism, **St. Peter Parish**)
  - Andrew Blair Carmichael – b. 5 Aug 1828, bapt. 19 Nov 1828 (Baptism, **St. Peter Parish**)

# Hurst

- o Hugh Richard Bond Carmichael, b. 21 Sep 1830, bapt. 10 Nov 1830 (Baptism, **St. Peter Parish**) & Mary Anne Coyne – 29 Mar 1853 (Marriage, **St. Mary Parish**)

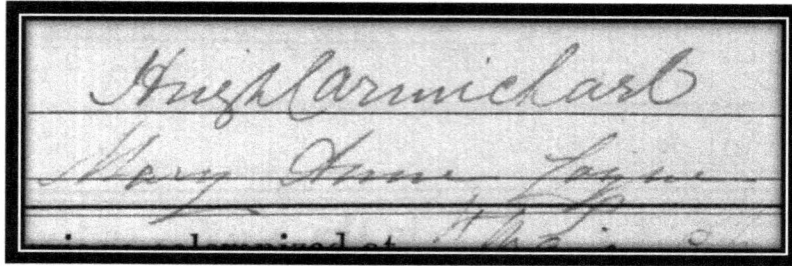

Signatures:

Hugh Carmichael (son):

   Residence - 2 Essex Bridge - March 29, 1853

   Occupation - Land Surveyor - March 29, 1853

Mary Anne Coyne, daughter of Christopher Coyne (daughter-in-law):

   Residence - Capel Street - March 29, 1853

   Relationship Status at Marriage - minor age

Christopher Coyne (father):

   Occupation - Letter

Andrew Blair Carmichael (father):

   Occupation - Solicitor

# Carmichael Surname Ireland: 1600s to 1900s

**Wedding Witnesses:**

**Christopher Coyne & Matilda Coyne**

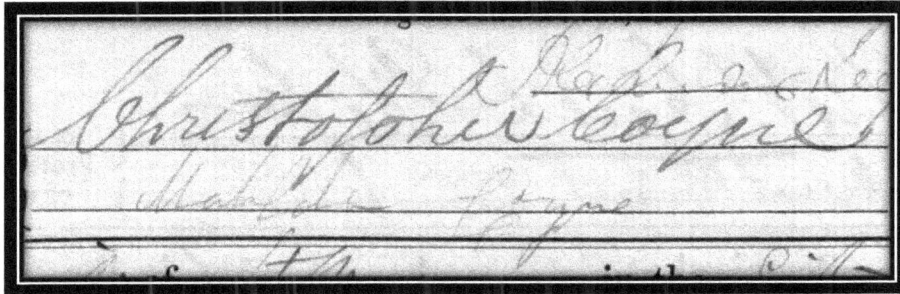

**Signatures:**

- Louisa Bourne Carmichael – b. 13 Oct 1833, bapt. 3 Dec 1833 (Baptism, **St. Peter Parish**), bur. 24 Feb 1848 (Burial, **St. Nicholas Without Parish**)

**Louisa Bourne Carmichael (daughter):**

**Residence - Temple Street - before February 24, 1848**

**Age at Death - 14 years**

- Walter Bourne Carmichael – b. 29 Jun 1835, bapt. 28 Aug 1835 (Baptism, **St. Peter Parish**), bur. 5 Sep 1853 (Burial, **St. Nicholas Without Parish**)

**Walter Bourne Carmichael (son):**

**Residence - Steven's Hospital - before September 5, 1853**

**Age at Death - 18 years**

- Richard Swift Carmichael – b. 11 May 1837, bapt. 14 Jul 1837 (Baptism, **St. Peter Parish**)

- Benjamin Pratt Swift – b. 12 Oct 1841, bapt. 16 Feb 1842 (Baptism, **St. Peter Parish**)

- Emily Christine Carmichael – b. Feb 1844, bapt. 11 Feb 1849 (Baptism, **St. Peter Parish**)

# Hurst

o   Elizabeth Jane Carmichael – b. 25 Jan 1847, bapt. 14 Feb 1848 (Baptism, **Clontarf Parish**)

**Andrew Blair Carmichael (father):**

Residence - St. Peter Parish - July 15, 1825

King's Street - November 19, 1828

August 28, 1835

French Street - December 3, 1833

39 French Street - July 14, 1837

November 10, 1830

Clontarf - February 14, 1848

No. 8 Ranelagh - February 16, 1842

Ranelagh - February 11, 1849

24 Rutland Square - before October 9, 1851

Occupation - Solicitor - February 16, 1842

February 14, 1848

February 11, 1849

Age at Death - 76 years

**Jane Swift (mother):**

Residence - St. Peter Parish - July 15, 1825

24 Rutland Square - before November 25, 1864

Age at Death - 69 years

# Carmichael Surname Ireland: 1600s to 1900s

**Wedding Witnesses:**

**Richard Swift & Saumareze Dubourdeau**

- Bridges John Carmichael & Frances Margaret Hooke

  o Bridges Carmichael – b. 21 Nov 1828, bapt. 6 Dec 1828 (Baptism, **Taney Parish**)

- Dennis Carmichael & Bridget Sohan

  o Margaret Carmichael – bapt. 23 Apr 1803 (Baptism, **SS. Michael & John Parish** (RC))

- Dennis Carmichael & Eleanor Dowling

  o John Carmichael – bapt. 6 Jul 1824 (Baptism, **St. Catherine Parish** (RC))

  o Thaddeus Carmichael – bapt. 17 Feb 1828 (Baptism, **St. Catherine Parish** (RC))

- Edward Carmichael & Agnes Coyle – 22 Jul 1845 (Marriage, **St. James Parish** (RC))

  o Mary Jane Carmichael – bapt. 7 Apr 1846 (Baptism, **St. James Parish** (RC))

- Edward Carmichael & M. Anne Donnelly – 21 Jul 1835 (Marriage, **St. James Parish** (RC))

  o John Carmichael – bapt. 30 Aug 1840 (Baptism, **St. James Parish** (RC))

**Wedding Witnesses:**

**John Dunne & William Carmichael**

- Edward Carmichael & Rose Mangan

  o John Carmichael – bapt. 21 May 1800 (Baptism, **St. Catherine Parish** (RC))

- Eugene Carmichael & Bridget Unknown

  o Margaret Carmichael – bapt. 1802 (Baptism, **St. Andrew Parish** (RC))

  o Elizabeth Carmichael – bapt. 1804 (Baptism, **St. Andrew Parish** (RC))

# Hurst

- Evory Carmichael & Margaret Carmichael

  - Thomas Carmichael – bapt. 13 Sep 1808 (Baptism, **St. Peter Parish**)

  - Evory Carmichael, bapt. 12 Jun 1811 (Baptism, **St. Mary Parish**) & Elizabeth O'Brien – 2 Sep 1836 (Marriage, **St. George Parish**)

**Signatures:**

- Rosalie Anne Carmichael – b. 26 Nov 1837, bapt. 24 Jan 1838 (Baptism, **St. Peter Parish**)

- Evory Thomas Carmichael – b. 21 Feb 1839, bapt. 3 May 1839 (Baptism, **St. Peter Parish**)

**Signatures:**

- Margaret Anderson Carmichael – b. 27 Aug 1840, bapt. 21 Oct 1840 (Baptism, **St. Peter Parish**)

- Evelyn Cecelia Carmichael – b. 7 Aug 1842, bapt. 30 Sep 1842 (Baptism, **St. Peter Parish**)

- Edith Elizabeth Carmichael – b. 13 Oct 1844, bapt. 18 Dec 1844 (Baptism, **St. Peter Parish**)

- George O'Brien Carmichael – b. 20 Dec 1846, bapt. 17 Mar 1847 (Baptism, **St. Peter Parish**)

# Carmichael Surname Ireland: 1600s to 1900s

Evory Carmichael (son):

    Residence - 18 Herbert Place, St. Peter Parish - September 2, 1836

        52 Fitzwilliam Place - January 24, 1838

            May 3, 1839

            October 21, 1840

            September 30, 1842

      Fitzwilliam Place - December 18, 1844

      42 Fitzwilliam Place - March 17, 1847

    Occupation - Private Gentleman - September 30, 1842

        Gentleman - December 18, 1844

        Esquire - March 17, 1847

Elizabeth O'Brien (daughter-in-law):

    Residence - Hardwick Street, St. George Parish - September 2, 1836

Wedding Witnesses:

George O'Brien & Thomas Carmichael

Signatures:

# Hurst

- o Henry Carmichael – b. 12 May 1816, bapt. 15 Mar 1817 (Baptism, **St. Peter Parish**)

- o Julie Carmichael, b. Dec 1817, bapt. 1 Oct 1819 (Baptism, **St. Peter Parish**) & Richard George Butcher – 7 Jul 1840 (Marriage, **St. Peter Parish**)

## Julie Carmichael (daughter):

Residence - Herbert Place - July 7, 1840

Occupation - Spinster - July 7, 1840

## Richard George Butcher (son-in-law):

Residence - Cork & Trinity College - July 7, 1840

Occupation - Butcher - July 7, 1840

## Wedding Witnesses:

Evory Carmichael & Anne Thomas

- o Margaret Carmichael & John Houston – 21 Jul 1841 (Marriage, **St. Peter Parish**)

## Margaret Carmichael (daughter):

Residence - Herbert Place - July 21, 1841

Occupation - Spinster - July 21, 1841

## John Houston (son-in-law):

Residence - York Street - July 21, 1841

Occupation - Esquire - July 21, 1841

## Wedding Witnesses:

Evory Carmichael & Thomas Edward Beatty

# Carmichael Surname Ireland: 1600s to 1900s

**Evory Carmichael (father):**

    Residence - Camden Street - September 13, 1808

- George Carmichael & Anne Butler

  - Mary Anne Carmichael – bapt. Jul 1781 (Baptism, **St. Nicholas Parish** (RC))

- George Carmichael & Bridget Unknown

  - George Carmichael & Honor Doran – 1 Oct 1876 (Marriage, **St. Catherine Parish** (RC))

    - Bridget Carmichael – b. 8 Jul 1877, bapt. 13 Jul 1877 (Baptism, **St. Nicholas Parish** (RC))

**George Carmichael (son):**

    Residence - Madden's Court - October 1, 1876

**Honor Doran, daughter of William Doran & Mary Unknown (daughter-in-law):**

    Residence - Madden's Court - October 1, 1876

- George Carmichael & Elizabeth Carmichael

  - John Carmichael – b. 5 May 1854, bapt. 2 Jun 1854 (Baptism, **St. George Parish**)

  - George Thomas Carmichael – b. 23 Oct 1855, bapt. 30 Nov 1855 (Baptism, **St. George Parish**)

**George Carmichael (father):**

    Residence - Eglinton, Cabra - June 2, 1854

        10 Lower Dominick Street - November 30, 1855

    Occupation - Solicitor - June 2, 1854

        November 30, 1855

# Hurst

- George Carmichael & Mary Anne Unknown

    - Mary Anne Carmichael – bapt. 1 Apr 1792 (Baptism, **St. Paul Parish**)

    - William Carmichael – bapt. 9 Jun 1794 (Baptism, **St. Paul Parish**)

    - Samuel Carmichael – bapt. 14 Apr 1799 (Baptism, **St. Catherine Parish**)

**George Carmichael (father):**

**Residence - Pool Street - April 14, 1799**

- Hugh Carmichael & Catherine Unknown

    - Catherine Lucy Anne Carmichael – b. 5 Feb 1842, bapt. 21 Feb 1842 (Baptism, **St. Nicholas Without Parish**)

**Hugh Carmichael (father):**

**Residence - 2 Harcourt Street - February 21, 1842**

**Occupation - Architecture - February 21, 1842**

- Hugh Carmichael & Mary Unknown

    - Hugh Christopher Carmichael – bapt. 10 Jan 1854 (Baptism, **SS. Michael & John Parish** (RC))

- Hugh Carmichael & Unknown

    - Anne Carmichael & John Cowan – 2 May 1771 (Marriage, **St. Bride Parish**)

**Anne Carmichael (daughter):**

**Residence - Bride Street - May 2, 1771**

**John Cowan (son-in-law):**

**Occupation - Merchant - May 2, 1771**

# Carmichael Surname Ireland: 1600s to 1900s

**Hugh Carmichael (father):**

    **Residence - Bride Street**

    **Occupation - Esquire**

- Hugh Carmichael & Unknown
  - Elizabeth Carmichael & Edward John Kittson – 16 Nov 1869 (Marriage, **St. Peter Parish**)

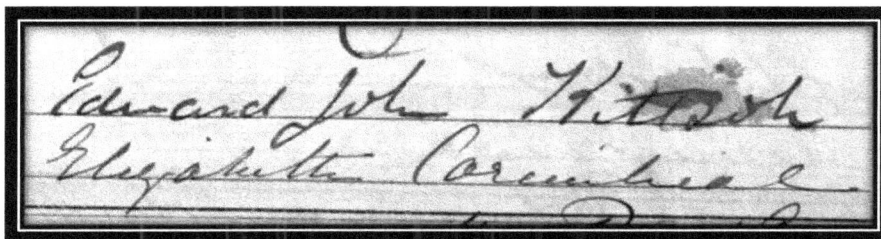

**Signatures:**

**Elizabeth Carmichael (daughter):**

    **Residence - 23 Lower Pembroke Street - November 16, 1869**

**Edward John Kittson, son of Francis Kittson (son-in-law):**

    **Residence - Hill View Terrace, Clontarf - November 16, 1869**

    **Occupation - Esquire, Medical Doctor - November 16, 1869**

**Francis Kittson (father):**

    **Occupation - Esquire**

**Hugh Carmichael (father):**

    **Occupation - Medical Doctor**

**Wedding Witnesses:**

Benjamin J. McDowell & Frances Kittson

**Signatures:**

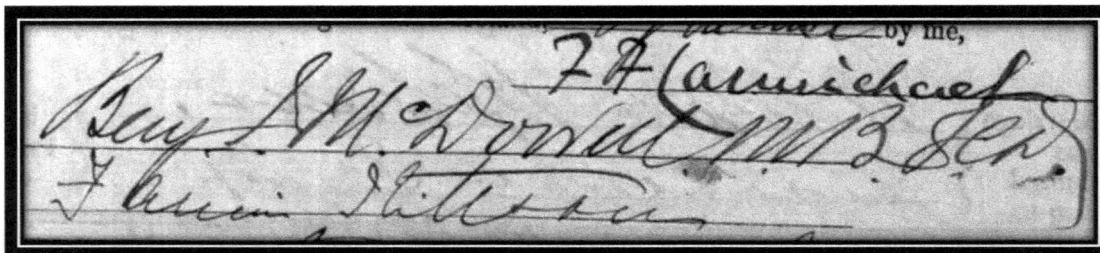

- J. Carmichael & Bridget Carmichael

  - Patrick Carmichael – b. 12 Jan 1896, bapt. 29 Jan 1896 (Baptism, **Rathmines Parish** (RC))

  - Anne Carmichael – b. 30 Jul 1898, bapt. 17 Aug 1898 (Baptism, **Rathmines Parish** (RC))

**J. Carmichael (father):**

Residence - 42 Ranelagh - January 29, 1896

Coombe Hospital - August 17, 1898

- James Carmichael & Catherine Carmichael

  - William Carmichael – bapt. 10 Dec 1766 (Baptism, **St. Michael Parish**)

**James Carmichael (father):**

Residence - Skinner Row - December 10, 1766

Occupation - Lace Weaver - December 10, 1766

# Carmichael Surname Ireland: 1600s to 1900s

- James Carmichael & Catherine Cotton – 31 Jun 1755 (Marriage, **St. Werburgh Parish**)

  o Valentine Carmichael – bapt. 10 May 1756 (Baptism, **St. Werburgh Parish**)

  o Mary Carmichael – bapt. 13 Nov 1757 (Baptism, **St. Werburgh Parish**)

  o Jane Carmichael – b. 1758, bur. 15 Jan 1761 (Burial, **St. Werburgh Parish**)

**Jane Carmichael (daughter):**

**Residence - Swan Alley - before January 15, 1761**

**Age at Death - 3 years**

**Cause of Death - smallpox**

  o Anne Carmichael – bapt. 20 Jun 1762 (Baptism, **St. Werburgh Parish**)

**James Carmichael (father):**

**Residence - Swan Alley - May 10, 1756**

**November 13, 1757**

**June 20, 1762**

# Hurst

- James Carmichael & Catherine Laurence – 4 May 1814 (Marriage, **St. Peter Parish**)

- James Carmichael & Elizabeth Carmichael

  - James Carmichael – b. 24 Jul 1835, bapt. 26 Sep 1835 (Baptism, **St. Peter Parish**)

  - Frederick Falkiner Carmichael & Susan Elizabeth Cotton – 7 May 1855 (Marriage, **St. Peter Parish**)

**Signatures:**

**Signatures (Marriage):**

# Carmichael Surname Ireland: 1600s to 1900s

- Lillian Zara Carmichael & Everard William Digby – 8 Oct 1885 (Marriage, **St. Peter Parish**)

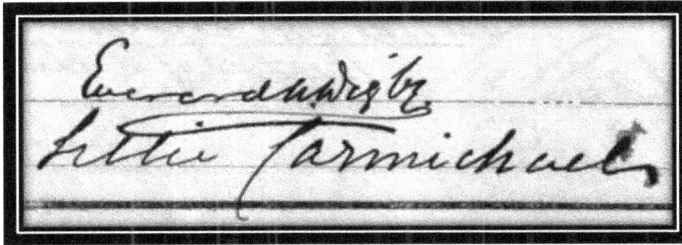

Signatures:

Lillian Zara Carmichael (daughter):

    Residence - 10 Sallymount Avenue, Ranelagh - October 8, 1885

Everard William Digby, son of William Arthur Digby (son-in-law):

    Residence - 47 Wellington Place, Clyde Road - October 8, 1885

    Occupation - Civil Engineer - October 8, 1885

William Athur Digby (father):

    Occupation - Gentleman

Frederick Falkiner Carmichael (father):

    Occupation - Clerk in Holy Orders

Wedding Witnesses:

Ninian M. Falkiner & James Dixon

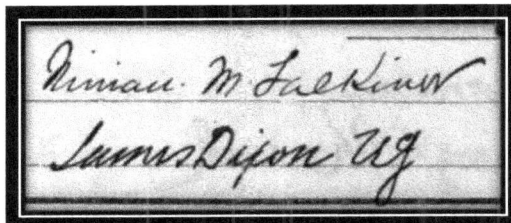

Signatures:

# Hurst

- Ethel Susan Carmichael, b. 12 Jan 1858, bapt. 21 Feb 1858 (Baptism, **St. Werburgh Parish**) & Joseph Hirste Haywood – 28 Dec 1886 (Marriage, **St. Peter Parish**)

Signature:

Signatures (Marriage):

Ethel Susan Carmichael (daughter):

Residence - 10 Sallymount Avenue, Ranelagh - December 28, 1886

Joseph Hirste Haywood, son of Joseph Haywood (son-in-law):

Residence - Fir Lodge College Sydenham, London - December 28, 1886

Occupation - Esquire - December 28, 1886

Joseph Haywood (father):

Occupation - Civil Engineer

Frederick Falkiner Carmichael (father):

Occupation - Clerk in Holy Orders

# Carmichael Surname Ireland: 1600s to 1900s

**Wedding Witnesses:**

James Dixon & J. C. Benson

**Signatures:**

- Eleanor Maude Carmichael, b. 7 Mar 1860, bapt. 22 Apr 1860 (Baptism, **St. Werburgh Parish**) &

  James Dixon, b. 1860 – 4 Aug 1891 (Marriage, **St. Peter Parish**)

**Signatures:**

**Signatures (Marriage):**

# Hurst

Eleanor Maude Carmichael (daughter):

    Residence - 10 Sallymount Avenue, Ranelagh - August 4, 1891

James Dixon, son of George Dixon (son-in-law):

    Residence - 17 Earlsfort Terrace - August 4, 1891

    Occupation - Merchant - August 4, 1891

George Dixon (father):

    Occupation - Merchant

Frederick Falkiner Carmichael (father):

    Occupation - Clerk in Holy Orders

Wedding Witnesses:

Stephen M. Dixon & Joseph Hirste Haywood

Signatures:

Frederick Falkner Carmichael (son):

    Residence - 87 Stephen's Green - May 7, 1855

        6 Clanbrassil Terrace - February 21, 1858

        89 Lower Leeson Street - April 22, 1860

# Carmichael Surname Ireland: 1600s to 1900s

Occupation - Esquire - May 7, 1855

Clerk - February 21, 1858

April 22, 1860

Susan Elizabeth Cotton, daughter of Francis Robert Cotton (daughter-in-law):

Residence - 6 Ushey, Ireland - May 7, 1855

Francis Robert Cotton (father):

Occupation - Gentleman

James Carmichael (father):

Occupation - Solicitor

Wedding Witnesses:

Frances A. Cotton & Jane N. Cotton

Signatures:

o   Emily Elizabeth Carmichael & Edward Arnold Carroll – 27 Apr 1859 (Marriage, **St. Peter Parish**)

Signatures:

Emily Elizabeth Carmichael (daughter):

Residence - 1 Prince Arthur Terrace, Rathmines - April 27, 1859

Edward Arnold Carroll, son of William Carroll (son-in-law):

Residence - 18 Elles Quay, St. Paul Parish - April 27, 1859

Occupation - Clerk in Holy Orders - April 27, 1859

William Carroll (father):

Occupation - Merchant

James Carmichael (father):

Occupation - Solicitor

# Carmichael Surname Ireland: 1600s to 1900s

**Wedding Witnesses:**

Frederick A. Carroll & Roger North

**Signatures:**

- o   William Carmichael – b. 4 Feb 1840, bapt. 29 May 1840 (Baptism, **St. Peter Parish**)

- o   Francis McClean Carmichael – b. 18 May 1841, bapt. 2 Jul 1841 (Baptism, **St. Peter Parish**)

- o   Olive Mary Carmichael, b. 24 May 1844, bapt. 14 Nov 1844 (Baptism, **St. Peter Parish**) & William Miles Lindsay – 18 Oct 1866 (Marriage, **St. Paul Parish**)

**Signatures:**

Olive Mary Carmichael (daughter):

Residence - 32 Arran Quay - October 18, 1866

William Miles Lindsay, son of James Lindsay (son-in-law):

Residence - 33 Bloomfield Avenue - October 18, 1866

Occupation - Clerk - October 18, 1866

James Lindsay (father):

Occupation - Merchant

# Hurst

James Carmichael (father):

Occupation - Solicitor

Wedding Witnesses:

Hugh Carmichael & Henry S. Halahan

Signatures:

- ○ Thomas Clarke Carmichael – b. 20 Oct 1846, bapt. 29 Apr 1847 (Baptism, **St. Peter Parish**)

- ○ Thomasina Eleanor Carmichael – b. 19 May 1848, bapt. 7 Nov 1848 (Baptism, **St. Peter Parish**)

- ○ Hartley Carmichael, b. 25 Apr 1854, bapt. 28 Jun 1854 (Baptism, **St. Peter Parish**) & Elizabeth Sarah Graham – 16 Oct 1879 (Marriage, **St. Peter Parish**)

Signatures:

Hartley Carmichael (son):

Residence - Whitwell Derbyshire - October 16, 1879

Occupation - Clerk in Holy Orders - October 16, 1879

Elizabeth Sarah Graham, daughter of Henry Torrens Graham (daughter-in-law):

Residence - 16 Charleston Terrace, Rathmines - October 16, 1879

Relationship Status at Marriage - minor

Henry Torrens Graham (father):

Occupation - Solicitor

James Carmichael (father):

Occupation - Clerk of the Crown

Wedding Witnesses:

Charles S. Graham & Ethel Carmichael

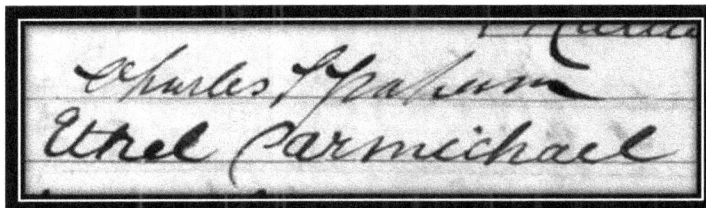

Signatures:

James Carmichael (father):

Residence - Stephen's Green - November 14, 1844

April 29, 1847

87 Stephen's Green - September 26, 1835

May 29, 1840

April 29, 1847

November 7, 1848

June 28, 1854

87 South Stephen's Green - July 2, 1841

# Hurst

Occupation - Solicitor - July 2, 1841

November 14, 1844

April 29, 1847

November 7, 1848

June 28, 1854

- James Carmichael & Elizabeth Carmichael
  - Anne Carmichael & John McGuinness – 7 Jul 1864 (Marriage, **St. Mary, Pro Cathedral Parish (RC)**)

Anne Carmichael (daughter):

Residence - 2 Hutton's Lane - July 7, 1864

John McGuinness, son of Daniel McGuinness & Bridget Unknown (son-in-law):

Residence - 8 Pim Street - July 7, 1864

- James Carmichael & Jane Carmichael
  - John Carmichael – bapt. 9 Jan1734 (Baptism, **St. Audoen Parish**)
- James Carmichael & Mary White – 1 Jun 1737 (Marriage, **St. Mary Parish**)
- James Carmichael & Philadelphia Holmes
  - Peter Carmichael – bapt. 16 Nov 1821 (Baptism, **St. Catherine Parish** (RC))
- James Carmichael & Roseanne Dunne
  - Anne Carmichael – bapt. 17 Oct 1836 (Baptism, **St. Nicholas Parish** (RC))
  - Elizabeth Carmichael (1st Marriage), bapt. 26 Jul 1841 (Baptism, **St. Nicholas Parish** (RC)) & Simon Walsh – 2 Nov 1868 (Marriage, **St. Michan Parish** (RC))

# Carmichael Surname Ireland: 1600s to 1900s

- James Walsh – b. 1878, bapt. 1878 (Baptism, **St. Andrew Parish** (RC))

o Elizabeth Carmichael Walsh (2<sup>nd</sup> Marriage), b. 26 Jul 1841 (Baptism, **St. Nicholas Parish** (RC)) &

John Cannon – 4 Sep 1881 (Marriage, **St. Andrew Parish** (RC))

**Elizabeth Carmichael Walsh (daughter):**

Residence - 10 Henrietta Place - November 2, 1868

170 Townsend Street - September 4, 1881

**Simon Walsh (1st Husband), son of Edward Walsh & Mary Unknown (son-in-law):**

Residence -10 Henrietta Place - November 2, 1868

3 Leeson Place - 1878

**John Cannon (2nd Husband), son of John Cannon (son-in-law):**

Residence - 19 Moss Street - September 4, 1881

- James Carmichael & Unknown

o Elizabeth Carmichael & Joseph Wilson – 25 Jun 1855 (Marriage, **St. Thomas Parish**)

**Signatures:**

**Elizabeth Carmichael (daughter):**

Residence - 42 Amiens Street - June 25, 1855

25

Joseph Wilson, son of Joseph Wilson (son-in-law):

> Residence - 42 Amiens Street - June 25, 1855

> Occupation - Law Clerk - June 25, 1855

Joseph Wilson (father):

> Occupation - Servant

James Carmichael (father):

> Occupation - Police Officer

Wedding Witnesses:

Joseph James & Robert Hooper

Signatures:

- James Carmichael & Unknown
  - Gulielmo Carmichael & Margaret Mooney – 26 Sep 1880 (Marriage, **St. James Parish (RC)**)

Gulielmo Carmichael (son):

> Residence - Park Gate Street - September 26, 1880

Margaret Mooney, daughter of Michael Mooney (daughter-in-law):

> Residence - 17 James Street - September 26, 1880

# Carmichael Surname Ireland: 1600s to 1900s

**Wedding Witnesses:**

**Christopher Mooney & Alice Langron**

- John Carmichael & Anne Carmichael
  - Roseanne Carmichael & Martin Doran – 20 May 1866 (Marriage, **St. Mary, Pro Cathedral Parish (RC)**)
    - Mary Doran – b. 13 Oct 1881, bapt. 17 Oct 1881 (Baptism, **St. Mary, Pro Cathedral Parish (RC)**)

**Roseanne Carmichael (daughter):**

Residence - **24 Britain Street** - May 20, 1866

**Martin Doran, son of Malachi Doran & Mary Unknown (son-in-law):**

Residence - **24 Great Britain Street** - May 20, 1866

**224 Great Britain Street** - October 17, 1881

**Wedding Witnesses:**

**Gulielmo Carmichael & Sarah Ambler**

- Mary Carmichael & James Tighe – 12 Jan 1868 (Marriage, **St. Mary, Pro Cathedral Parish (RC)**)

**Mary Carmichael (daughter):**

Residence - **210 Britain Street** - January 12, 1868

**James Tighe, son of Martin Tighe & Esther Unknown (son-in-law):**

Residence - **89 Britain Street** - January 12, 1868

# Hurst

**Wedding Witnesses:**

**Martin Doran & Roseanne Doran**

- John Carmichael & Bridget Anne Ryan

    o Francis Carmichael – b. 1873, bapt. 1873 (Baptism, **Saggart Parish (RC)**)

    o Lawrence Carmichael – b. 1874, bapt. 1874 (Baptism, **Saggart Parish (RC)**)

    o Richard Carmichael – b. 1876, bapt. 1876 (Baptism, **Saggart Parish (RC)**)

    o Patrick Carmichael & Mary Davis – 30 Apr 1899 (Marriage, **St. Mary, Pro Cathedral Parish (RC)**)

**Patrick Carmichael (son):**

**Residence - 43 Crampton Buildings - April 30, 1899**

**Mary Davis, daughter of Patrick Davis & Elizabeth Doyle (daughter-in-law):**

**Residence - 75 Middle Abbey Street - April 30, 1899**

**Wedding Witnesses:**

**Edward Doyle & Mary Doyle**

**John Carmichael (father):**

**Residence - Rathcoole - 1873**

**1874**

**1876**

- John Carmichael & Eleanor Carmichael

    o James Carmichael – bapt. 28 Mar 1781 (Baptism, **St. Luke Parish**)

    o George Carmichael – bapt. 23 Jul 1783 (Baptism, **St. Luke Parish**)

# Carmichael Surname Ireland: 1600s to 1900s

**John Carmichael (father):**

Residence - Skinner's Alley - March 28, 1781

July 23, 1783

Occupation - Hosier - March 28, 1781

Stocking Maker - July 23, 1783

- John Carmichael & Hannah Carmichael, bur. 26 Aug 1733 (Burial, **St. Luke Parish**)
  - Henry Carmichael – bapt. 5 Jan 1720 (Baptism, **St. Luke Parish**)
  - John Carmichael – bapt. 24 Jun 1722 (Baptism, **St. Luke Parish**), bur. 13 Aug 1723 (Burial, **St. Luke Parish**)

**John Carmichael (son):**

Cause of Death - teeth

  - James Carmichael – bapt. 21 Nov 1723 (Baptism, **St. Luke Parish**)
  - Abraham Carmichael – bapt. 21 Jun 1725 (Baptism, **St. Luke Parish**), bur. 23 Jun 1725 (Burial, **St. Luke Parish**)

**Abraham Carmichael (son):**

Age at Death - infant

  - John Carmichael – bapt. 11 Feb 1728 (Baptism, **St. Luke Parish**)
  - George Carmichael – bapt. 9 Feb 1729 (Baptism, **St. Luke Parish**), bur. 30 Sep 1730 (Burial, **St. Luke Parish**)
  - Hannah Carmichael – bur. 19 Jun 1733 (Burial, **St. Luke Parish**)

# Hurst

**Hannah Carmichael (daughter):**

    **Cause of Death - Teeth**

      ○  Mary Carmichael – bur. 1 Jan 1737 (Burial, **St. Luke Parish**)

**John Carmichael (father):**

    **Residence - Coombe - January 5, 1720**

                  **November 21, 1723**

           **Lower Coombe - June 24, 1722**

    **Occupation - Hosier - January 5, 1720**

                  **November 21, 1723**

           **Stocking Weaver – June 24, 1722**

**Hannah Carmichael (mother):**

    **Cause of Death - consumption**

- John Carmichael & Jane Amelia Carmichael
  - ○ Jane Amelia Carmichael (1st Marriage), b. 24 May 1825, bapt. 11 Jun 1825 (Baptism, **St. George Parish**) & John Parr – 2 Jun 1857 (Marriage, **St. George Parish**)

**Signatures:**

# Carmichael Surname Ireland: 1600s to 1900s

Jane Amelia Carmichael (daughter):

   Residence - 7 Upper Temple Street - June 2, 1857

John Parr (1st Husband), son of John George Parr (son-in-law):

   Residence - Clones, Co. Monaghan - June 2, 1857

      7 Upper Temple Street - June 2, 1857

   Occupation - Solicitor - June 2, 1857

John George Parr (father):

   Occupation - Esquire

John Carmichael (father):

   Occupation - Solicitor

Wedding Witnesses:

Thomas Carmichael & William Moore

Signatures:

# Hurst

- Jane Amelia Carmichael Parr (2<sup>nd</sup> Marriage), b. 24 May 1825, bapt. 11 Jun 1825 (Baptism, **St. George Parish**) & Elliot Motherwell – 6 Aug 1873 (Marriage, **Clontarf Parish**)

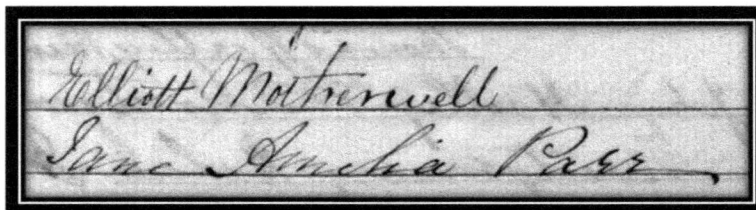

Signatures:

Jane Amelia Carmichael Parr (daughter):

Residence - 4 Victoria Lee, Clontarf - August 6, 1873

Relationship Status at Marriage - widow

Elliot Motherwell (2<sup>nd</sup> Husband), son of Maiben C. Motherwell (son-in-law):

Residence - 2 Victoria Lee, Clontarf - August 6, 1873

Occupation - Esquire - August 6, 1873

Maiben C. Motherwell (father):

Occupation - Clerk

John Carmichael (father):

Occupation - Solicitor

# Carmichael Surname Ireland: 1600s to 1900s

**Wedding Witnesses:**

Wyndham Guinness, James Williams, J. A. Carmichael, & Leticia Louisa Carmichael

**Signatures:**

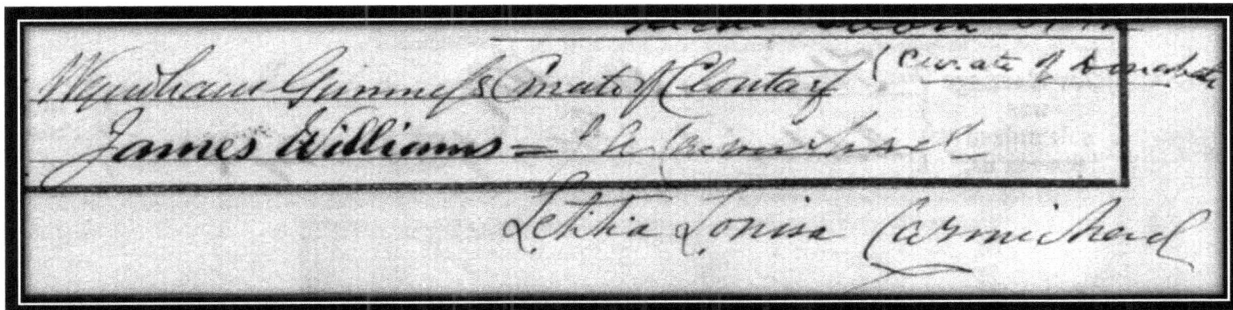

o   George Carmichael, b. 1 Jan 1827, bapt. 3 Feb 1827 (Baptism, **St. George Parish**) & Elizabeth Baker

   Erskine – 4 Aug 1853 (Marriage, **St. George Parish**)

**Signatures:**

**George Carmichael (son):**

   Residence - 7 Upper Temple Street - August 4, 1853

   Occupation - Esquire - August 4, 1853

**Elizabeth Baker Erskine, daughter of Robert Baker (daughter-in-law):**

   Residence - Cabra Parade, Grange Gorman Parish - August 4, 1853

   Relationship Status at Marriage - widow

# Hurst

**Robert Baker (father):**

Occupation - Esquire

**John Carmichael (father):**

Occupation - Solicitor

**Wedding Witnesses:**

**Isaac Baker & Robert Carmichael**

**Signatures:**

o   Robert Bell Booth Carmichael – b. 9 Oct 1828, bapt. 2 Nov 1830 (Baptism, **St. George Parish**)

**Signatures:**

o   Mary Carmichael – b. 2 Jul 1830, bapt. 14 Sep 1830 (Baptism, **St. George Parish**)

**John Carmichael (father):**

Residence - No. 7 Temple Street - February 3, 1827

September 14, 1830

November 2, 1830

Occupation - Solicitor - February 3, 1827

# Carmichael Surname Ireland: 1600s to 1900s

### September 14, 1830

### November 2, 1830

- John Carmichael & Leticia Myrth – 2 Jun 1793 (Marriage, **St. Michan Parish**)

**John Carmichael (husband):**

Residence - St. Michan Parish - June 2, 1793

**Leticia Myrth (wife):**

Residence - St. Michan Parish - June 2, 1793

- John Carmichael & Margaret Tracey
  - John Carmichael – bapt. 29 Jun 1822 (Baptism, **Cork - South Parish (RC)**)
- John Carmichael & Mary Grainvile – 30 Nov 1733 (Marriage, **St. Bride Parish**)
  - Elizabeth Carmichael – bur. 4 Sep 1735 (Burial, **St. Luke Parish**)
- John Carmichael & Mary Monks
  - John Carmichael – bapt. 1833 (Baptism, **Clondalkin Parish (RC)**)
- John Carmichael & Mary Unknown
  - Eleanor Carmichael – bur. 17 Sep 1731 (Burial, **St. Mary Parish**)
  - Mary Carmichael – bur. 8 Jan 1736 (Burial, **St. Mary Parish**)
- John Carmichael & Mary Unknown
  - Mary Carmichael – bapt. 12 Sep 1798 (Baptism, **St. Nicholas Without Parish**)

**John Carmichael (father):**

Residence - Francis Street - September 12, 1798

- John Carmichael & Susan Farrant – 30 Oct 1786 (Marriage, **Cork - SS. Peter & Paul Parish (RC)**)

- John Carmichael & Unknown

  - Mary Carmichael – bur. 3 Dec 1740 (Burial, **St. Luke Parish**)

- John Carmichael & Unknown

  - Robert Carmichael & Mary Blunt Porter – 12 Oct 1862 (Marriage, **St. Mark Parish**)

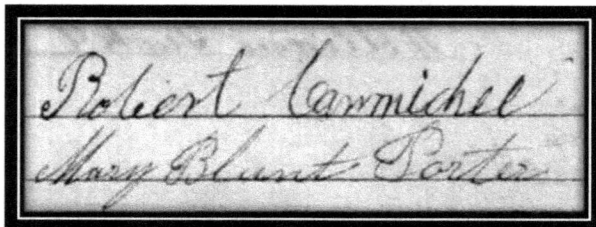

**Signatures:**

- Frances Eleanor Carmichael – b. 23 May 1864, bapt. 5 Jun 1864 (Baptism, **St. Mark Parish**)

**Robert Carmichael (son):**

**Residence - The Barque "Ocean Pride" (A Ship) - October 12, 1862**

**32 Sir John's Quay - June 5, 1864**

**Occupation - Sailor - October 12, 1862**

**June 5, 1864**

**Mary Blunt Porter, daughter of Samuel Porter (daughter-in-law):**

**Residence - 32 Sir John Rogerson's Quay - October 12, 1862**

**Samuel Porter (father):**

**Occupation - Master Mariner**

**John Carmichael (father):**

**Occupation - Stone Mason**

**Wedding Witnesses:**

Joseph Ryan & Bernard Kavanagh

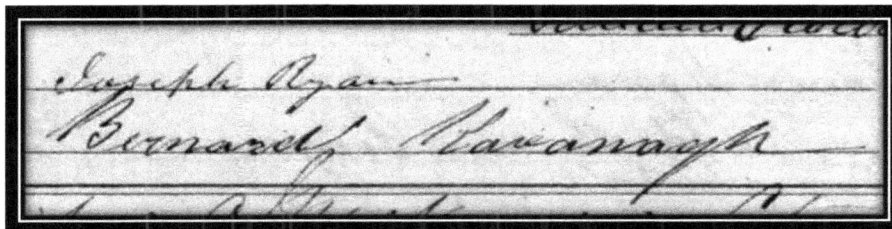

**Signatures:**

- John Carmichael & Wilhelmina Unknown

  o   Mary Margaret Carmichael – bapt. 1850 (Baptism, **Clondalkin Parish (RC)**)

  o   Elizabeth Carmichael – bapt. 1854 (Baptism, **Clondalkin Parish (RC)**)

- John Valentine Carmichael & Jane Mary Unknown

  o   Elizabeth Carmichael – bapt. 14 May 1732 (Baptism, **St. Werburgh Parish**)

  o   Valentine Carmichael – bapt. Nov 1734 (Baptism, **St. Werburgh Parish**)

  o   James Carmichael – bapt. 31 Jan 1739 (Baptism, **St. Werburgh Parish**)

**John Valentine Carmichael (father):**

Residence - Castle Street - May 14, 1732

November 1734

January 31, 1739

- John Wilson Carmichael & Mary Jane Carmichael

  o   Louisa Carmichael – b. 14 Jan 1872, bapt. 13 Feb 1876 (Baptism, **St. Barnabas Parish**)

  o   William Robert Carmichael – b. 2 Jan 1874, bapt. 13 Feb 1876 (Baptism, **St. Barnabas Parish**)

  o   Elizabeth Carmichael – b. 3 Nov 1875, bapt. 13 Feb 1876 (Baptism, **St. Barnabas Parish**)

# Hurst

*John Wilson Carmichael (father):*

Residence - 7 Oxford Terrace - February 13, 1876

Occupation - Officer of Customs - February 13, 1876

- Joseph Carmichael & Jane Unknown

  o Mary Carmichael – bapt. 23 Mar 1788 (Baptism, **St. Nicholas Parish (RC)**)

- Lawrence Carmichael & Mary Sullivan

  o Catherine Carmichael & Edward Mooney – 30 Oct 1892 (Marriage, **St. Mary, Pro Cathedral Parish (RC)**)

*Catherine Carmichael (daughter):*

Residence - 40 Cole's Lane - October 30, 1892

*Edward Mooney, son of Edward Mooney & Margaret Carroll (son-in-law):*

Residence - 40 Cole's Lane - October 30, 1892

- Lloyd Carmichael & Unknown

Signature:

  o Edith Elizabeth Frances Carmichael – b. 21 Sep 1898, bapt. 23 Oct 1898 (Baptism, **Dromod & Prior Parish**)

  o Grace Marguerite Carmichael – b. 6 Jul 1900, bapt. 29 Jul 1900 (Baptism, **Dromod & Prior Parish**)

# Carmichael Surname Ireland: 1600s to 1900s

**Lloyd Carmichael (father):**

    Residence - Waterville - October 12, 1898

                July 29, 1900

    Occupation - Telegraphist - October 12, 1898

                July 29, 1900

- Moynard Carmichael & Anne Redmond
  - Frederick Joseph Carmichael – b. 13 May 1896, bapt. 22 May 1896 (Baptism, **Harrington Street Parish** (RC))

**Moynard Carmichael (father):**

    Residence - 2 Charlemont Mall - May 22, 1896

- Owen Matthew Carmichael & Anne Spratt – 17 Sep 1775 (Marriage, **St. Catherine Parish** (RC))
  - Owen Carmichael – bapt. 1 Oct 1777 (Baptism, **St. Catherine Parish** (RC))
  - Catherine Carmichael – bapt. 11 Mar 1781 (Baptism, **St. Catherine Parish** (RC))

**Wedding Witnesses:**

**Bridget Spratt & Mary Andrews**

- Owen Carmichael & Bridget Reilly
  - William Carmichael – bapt. 1 Feb 1808 (Baptism, **St. Mary, Pro Cathedral Parish** (RC))
  - Mary Carmichael – bapt. 16 Apr 1810 (Baptism, **St. Mary, Pro Cathedral Parish** (RC))
- Patrick Carmichael & Margaret Unknown
  - Rose Carmichael – bapt. 26 Jul 1749 (Baptism, **St. Mary, Pro Cathedral Parish** (RC))

# Hurst

- Patrick Carmichael & Mary Carmichael

  - Melissa Carmichael – bapt. 24 Jul 1835 (Baptism, **St. Mary, Pro Cathedral Parish (RC)**)

- Patrick Carmichael & Mary Davis

  - Bridget Mary Carmichael – b. 1900, bapt. 1900 (Baptism, **St. Andrew Parish (RC)**)

## Patrick Carmichael (father):

### Residence - Holles Street Hospital - 1900

- Richard Carmichael & Jane Bourne (B o u r n e) – 10 Nov 1812 (Marriage, **St. Peter Parish**)

- Richard Freeman Carmichael & Catherine Jane Carmichael

  - Reginald William Carmichael – b. 12 Jul 1871, bapt. 7 Nov 1871 (Baptism, **Molyneux Chapel Parish**)

  - Florence Maude Carmichael – b. 24 Apr 1873, bapt. 10 Aug 1873 (Baptism, **Irishtown Parish**)

  - Edith Jane Carmichael – b. 13 Dec 1875, bapt. 6 Feb 1876 (Baptism, **St. George Parish**)

  - Anne Freeman Carmichael – b. 3 Jan 1878, bapt. 16 Jan 1878 (Baptism, **St. George Parish**)

## Richard Freeman Carmichael (father):

### Residence - 95 Lower Mount Street - November 7, 1871

### 47 Tritonville Road - August 10, 1873

### 3 Russell Terrace, Jones Road - February 6, 1876

### 2 Norman Villas - January 16, 1878

### Occupation - Gentleman - November 7, 1871

### Clerk in Bank of Ireland - August 10, 1873

### February 6, 1876

# Carmichael Surname Ireland: 1600s to 1900s

**Bank Clerk - January 16, 1878**

- Robert Carmichael & Elizabeth Carmichael

  o   Anne Carmichael – bapt. 5 Aug 1770 (Baptism, **St. Mary Parish**)

  o   William Carmichael – b. 1771, bapt. 29 Sep 1771 (Baptism, **St. Mary Parish**)

  o   Robert Carmichael – bapt. 6 Feb 1774 (Baptism, **St. Mary Parish**)

**Robert Carmichael (father):**

**Residence - Prince's Street - August 5, 1770**

**September 29, 1771**

**Moore Street - February 6, 1774**

- Robert Carmichael & Elizabeth Carmichael

  o   Susan Carmichael – bapt. 12 Nov 1780 (Baptism, **St. Luke Parish**)

  o   Robert Carmichael – bapt. 17 Mar 1782 (Baptism, **St. Luke Parish**)

**Robert Carmichael (father):**

**Residence - Fordhams Alley - November 12, 1780**

**March 17, 1782**

**Occupation - Hosier - November 12, 1780**

**Weaver - March 17, 1782**

- Robert Carmichael & Elizabeth Unknown

  o   Jane Carmichael – bapt. 23 Nov 1760 (Baptism, **St. Nicholas Without Parish**)

# Hurst

**Robert Carmichael (father):**

### Residence - Arrundale Court - November 23, 1760

- Robert Carmichael & Elizabeth Unknown
  - Elizabeth Carmichael – bapt. 3 May 1763 (Baptism, **St. Catherine Parish**)
  - Mary Carmichael – bapt. 12 Aug 1764 (Baptism, **St. Catherine Parish**)
  - John Carmichael – bapt. 22 Jun 1766 (Baptism, **St. Audoen Parish**)

**Robert Carmichael (father):**

### Residence - Elbow Lane - August 12, 1764

- Robert Carmichael & Frances Carmichael
  - Elizabeth Carmichael – bapt. 22 May 1803 (Baptism, **St. Paul Parish**)
- Robert Carmichael & Mary Flynn
  - Robert John Carmichael – b. 27 Apr 1877, bapt. 7 May 1877 (Baptism, **St. Agatha Parish** (RC))

**Robert Carmichael (father):**

### Residence - 19 Portland Street - May 7, 1877

- Robert Carmichael & Unknown
  - William John Carmichael & Mary Nicholson – 21 Feb 1887 (Marriage, **St. Mark Parish**)

**Signatures:**

# Carmichael Surname Ireland: 1600s to 1900s

**William John Carmichael (son):**

    Residence - 5 Norman Villas, Jones Road, Dublin - February 21, 1887

    Occupation - Miller - February 21, 1887

**Mary Nicholson, daughter of John Nicholson (daughter-in-law):**

    Residence - 23 East Hanover Street, Dublin - February 21, 1887

**John Nicholson (father):**

    Occupation - Foreman in Gas Work

**Robert Carmichael (father):**

    Occupation - Stone Clerk

**Wedding Witnesses:**

**William Henry Ash & Jane Nicholson Steel**

**Signatures:**

- Samuel Carmichael & Milley Carmichael
  - Andrew Carmichael – b. 12 Nov 1787, bapt. 21 Dec 1787 (Baptism, **Carlow Parish**)
  - Samuel Christmas Carmichael – b. 25 Jan 1789, bapt. 13 Jan 1790 (Baptism, **Carlow Parish**)
- Singleton Carmichael & Anne McClair
  - Elizabeth Carmichael – b. 5 May 1862, bapt. 28 May 1862 (Baptism, **St. Nicholas Parish** (RC))

# Hurst

**Singleton Carmichael (father):**

**Residence - 14 Arthur's Lane - May 28, 1862**

- Terrence Carmichael & Catherine Unknown
  - Patrick Carmichael – b. 1765, bapt. 1765 (Baptism, **SS. Michael & John Parish** (RC))
- Thomas Carmichael & Abigail Susan Unknown (1st Marriage)
  - Evory Carmichael – b. 4 Jan 1832, bapt. 2 Feb 1832 (Baptism, **St. Peter Parish**)
  - William Edward Carmichael – b. 7 Apr 1841, bapt. 5 May 1841 (Baptism, **St. Peter Parish**)

**Thomas Carmichael (father):**

**Residence - 41 Camden Street - February 2, 1832**

**11 Lower Baggot Street - May 5, 1841**

**Occupation - Clergyman - May 5, 1841**

- Abigail Susan Unknown Car Michael (2nd Marriage) & John Cotter Gregg – 23 May 1844 (Marriage, **St. Peter Parish**)

**Abigail Susan Unknown Carmichael (wife):**

**Residence - 41 Stephen's Green East - May 23, 1844**

**Relationship Status at Marriage - widow**

**John Cotter Gregg (husband):**

**Residence - 82 Dame Street, St. Andrew Parish - May 23, 1844**

**Occupation - Gentleman - May 23, 1844**

# Carmichael Surname Ireland: 1600s to 1900s

**Wedding Witnesses:**

**Arthur Yates Bundt & S. Ryan Troy**

- Thomas Carmichael & Mary Carroll

    o Mary Margaret Carmichael – b. 1872, bapt. 1872 (Baptism, **St. Andrew Parish** (RC))

    o Catherine Mary Josephine Carmichael – b. 1877, bapt. 1877 (Baptism, **St. Andrew Parish** (RC))

**Thomas Carmichael (father):**

**Residence - 39 Aungier Street - 1872**

**18 Molesworth Street - 1877**

- Unknown Carmichael & Bridget Carmichael

    o Mary Frances Carmichael – b. 26 Jan 1894, bapt. 31 Jan 1894 (Baptism, **St. Mary, Pro Cathedral Parish** (RC))

**Unknown Carmichael (father):**

**Residence - Rotunda Hospital - January 31, 1894**

- Unknown Carmichael & Mary Carmichael

    o George Carmichael – bur. 26 Jul 1723 (Burial, **St. Mary Parish**)

- Unknown Carmichael & Unknown

    o B. G. Carmichael

**Signature:**

- Unknown Carmichael & Unknown

  - Elizabeth Carmichael

**Signature:**

- Unknown Carmichael & Unknown

  - Hugh Carmichael

**Signature:**

- Unknown Carmichael & Unknown

  - Hugh Carmichael

**Signature:**

- Unknown Carmichael & Unknown

  - Hugh Carmichael

**Signature:**

- Unknown Carmichael & Unknown

  o Richard Carmichael

**Signature:**

- Unknown Carmichael & Unknown

  o Robert Carmichael

**Signature:**

- Unknown Carmichael & Unknown

  o Robert Carmichael

**Signature:**

- William Carmichael & Catherine Rollings – 30 Sep 1822 (Marriage, **St. James Parish**)

**Signatures:**

- William Carmichael & Elizabeth Carmichael

  o Benjamin Carmichael – b. 15 Apr 1824, bapt. 16 May 1824 (Baptism, **St. George Parish**)

- William Carmichael & Elizabeth Lyons – 9 Apr 1844 (Marriage, **St. James Parish** (RC))

- William Carmichael & Jane Farrell – 24 Oct 1852 (Marriage, **St. Andrew Parish** (RC))

- William Carmichael & Lucy Unknown

  o Margaret Carmichael – bapt. 1854 (Baptism, **St. Andrew Parish** (RC))

- William Carmichael & Mary Allen

  o William Carmichael – bapt. 3 Apr 1780 (Baptism, **St. Catherine Parish** (RC))

- William Carmichael & Mary Joyce – 22 Aug 1797 (Marriage, **St. Bride Parish**)

**William Carmichael (husband):**

**Occupation - Silk Merchant - August 22, 1797**

- William Carmichael & Unknown

  o Margaret Carmichael & Thomas McManus – 21 Nov 1880 (Marriage, **St. Mary Parish**)

**Signatures:**

# Carmichael Surname Ireland: 1600s to 1900s

**Margaret Carmichael (daughter):**

    Residence - 2 Upper Abbey Street - November 21, 1880

**Thomas McManus, son of Joseph McManus (son-in-law):**

    Residence - 2 Upper Abbey Street - November 21, 1880

    Occupation - Porter - November 21, 1880

**Joseph McManus (father):**

    Occupation - Traveller

**William Carmichael (father):**

    Occupation - Cage Maker

**Wedding Witnesses:**

**Frederick Ludlow & Elizabeth McManus**

**Signatures:**

# Hurst

# Individual Baptisms/Births

- Unknown Carmichael – bapt. Unclear (Baptism, **St. Paul Parish**)

# Individual Burials

- Andrew Carmichael – b. 1796, bur. 5 Apr 1848 (Burial, **St. Nicholas Without Parish**)

Andrew Carmichael (deceased):

   Residence - Temple Street - before April 5, 1848

   Age at Death - 52 years

- Andrew Blair Carmichael – b. 1783, bur. 16 Apr 1821 (Burial, **St. Nicholas Without Parish**)

Andrew Blair Carmichael (deceased):

   Residence - Mount Pleasant - before April 16, 1821

   Age at Death - 38 years

- Anne Carmichael – b. 1747, bur. 10 Aug 1819 (Burial, **St. Peter Parish**)

Anne Carmichael (deceased):

   Residence - White Friar Lane - before August 10, 1819

   Age at Death - 72 years

- Benjamin Carmichael – b. May 1825, bur. 16 Sep 1825 (Burial, **St. George Parish**)

Benjamin Carmichael (deceased):

   Age at Death - 5 Months

# Carmichael Surname Ireland: 1600s to 1900s

- Benjamin Carmichael – b. 1842, bur. 12 Jul 1849 (Burial, **St. Nicholas Without Parish**)

**Benjamin Carmichael (deceased):**

> **Residence - Camden Place - before July 12, 1849**

> **Age at Death - 7 years**

- Catherine Carmichael – bur. 11 Nov 1827 (Burial, **St. Nicholas Without Parish**)

**Catherine Carmichael (deceased):**

> **Residence - Stephen's Green - before November 11, 1827**

- Daniel Carmichael – bur. 20 Aug 1779 (Burial, **St. Paul Parish**)
- Edmond Carmichael – b. 1812, bur. 30 Apr 1816 (Burial, **St. Peter Parish**)

**Edmond Carmichael (deceased):**

> **Residence - Stephen's Green - before April 30, 1816**

> **Age at Death - 4 years**

- Edward Carmichael – b. 1821, d. 30 May 1849, bur. 30 May 1849 (Burial, **Arbour Hill Barracks Parish**)

**Edward Carmichael (deceased):**

> **Residence - Arbour Hill Barracks - May 30, 1849**

> **Occupation - Private in 2nd Regiment - May 30, 1849**

> **Age at Death - 28 years**

> **Cause of Death - cholera**

# Hurst

- Eleanor Lloyd Carmichael – b. 1805, bur. 6 Apr 1829 (Burial, **St. George Parish**)

Eleanor Lloyd Carmichael (deceased):

    Residence - Frederick Street - before April 6, 1829

    Age at Death - 24 years

- Elizabeth Carmichael – bur. 9 Oct 1826 (Burial, **St. George Parish**)

Elizabeth Carmichael (deceased):

    Residence - St. Mary Parish - before October 9, 1826

    Relationship Status at Death - Miss

- Frederick Carmichael – b. 1818, bur. 1 Feb 1854 (Burial, **St. Nicholas Without Parish**)

Frederick Carmichael (deceased):

    Residence - Bolton Street - before February 1, 1854

    Age at Death - 36 years

- Frederick Bonsfield Carmichael – b. 1812, bur. 14 Jul 1834 (Burial, **St. Paul Parish**)

Frederick Bonsfield Carmichael (deceased):

    Age at Death - 22 years

- Henry Carmichael – b. 1816, bur. 21 Mar 1817 (Burial, **St. Peter Parish**)

Henry Carmichael (deceased):

    Residence - St. Peter Parish - before March 21, 1817

    Age at Death - 1 year

# Carmichael Surname Ireland: 1600s to 1900s

- Hugh Carmichael – b. 1848, bur. May 1849 (Burial, **St. Nicholas Without Parish**)

## Hugh Carmichael (deceased):

Residence - Stephen's Green - before May 1849

Age at Death - 1 year

- Isabel Carmichael – b. 1749, bur. 15 Mar 1814 (Burial, **St. Catherine Parish**)

## Isabel Carmichael (deceased):

Residence - Cole Alley - before March 15, 1814

Age at Death - 65 years

- James Carmichael – bur. 25 Feb 1755 (Burial, **St. Paul Parish**)
- James Carmichael – bur. 26 Mar 1781 (Burial, **St. Nicholas Without Parish**)
- James Carmichael – bur. 24 May 1814 (Burial, **St. Mark Parish**)

## James Carmichael (deceased):

Residence - Eden Quay - before May 24, 1814

- Jane Carmichael – bur. 17 Jul 1776 (Burial, **St. Paul Parish**)
- Jane Carmichael – b. 1792, bur. 10 Feb 1832 (Burial, **St. Nicholas Without Parish**)

## Jane Carmichael (deceased):

Residence - Stephen's Green - before February 10, 1832

Age at Death - 40 years

# Hurst

- Jane Carmichael – b. 1752, bur. 18 Oct 1836 (Burial, **St. Nicholas Without Parish**)

Jane Carmichael (deceased):

Residence - Henry Street - before October 18, 1836

Age at Death - 84 years

- Jane Carmichael – b. 1811, bur. 11 May 1848 (Burial, **St. Nicholas Without Parish**)

Jane Carmichael (deceased):

Residence - Summerhill Parish - before May 11, 1848

Age at Death - 37 years

- Jane Carmichael – b. 1817, bur. 8 Jun 1849 (Burial, **St. Nicholas Without Parish**)

Jane Carmichael (deceased):

Residence - Closter Palace - before June 8, 1849

Age at Death - 32 years

- John Carmichael – bur. 18 Nov 1804 (Burial, **St. Paul Parish**)
- Joseph Carmichael – b. 1785, bur. 16 Feb 1818 (Burial, **St. Peter Parish**)

Joseph Carmichael (deceased):

Residence - Clarendon Street - before February 16, 1818

Age at Death - 33 years

# Carmichael Surname Ireland: 1600s to 1900s

- Margaret Carmichael (Child) – bur. 12 Nov 1737 (Burial, **St. Paul Parish**)

- Margaret Carmichael – bur. 6 Jan 1804 (Burial, **St. Paul Parish**)

- Margaret Carmichael – b. 1765, d. 5 May 1825, bur. 5 May 1825 (Burial, **St. Catherine Parish**) (Burial, **St. Catherine Parish (RC)**)

**Margaret Carmichael (deceased):**

  **Residence - Coombe - May 5, 1825**

  **Age at Death - 60 years**

- Mary Carmichael – bur. 7 Jan 1728 (Burial, **St. Catherine Parish**)

**Mary Carmichael (deceased):**

  **Age at Death - child**

- Mary Carmichael – bur. 17 Jul 1734 (Burial, **St. Catherine Parish**)

**Mary Carmichael (deceased):**

  **Relationship Status at Death - widow**

- Mary Carmichael – bur. 23 Dec 1734 (Burial, **St. Mary Parish**)

- Mary Carmichael – bur. 27 Apr 1738 (Burial, **St. Luke Parish**)

- Mary Carmichael – bur. 20 Jan 1768 (Burial, **St. James Parish**)

**Mary Carmichael (deceased):**

  **Residence - Barrack Street - before January 20, 1768**

- Mary Carmichael – bur. 17 Sep 1811 (Burial, **St. Peter Parish**)

**Mary Carmichael (deceased):**

**Residence - Stephen's Green - before September 17, 1811**

**Place of Burial - St. Kevin's Cemetery**

- Nicholas Carmichael  – bur. 18 May 1738 (Burial, **St. Catherine Parish**)

- Peter Carmichael – bur. 9 Jun 1761 (Burial, **St. Paul Parish**)

- Rebecca Carmichael – b. Apr 1821, bur. 7 Sep 1825 (Burial, **St. George Parish**)

**Rebecca Carmichael (deceased):**

**Age at Death - 4 ½ years**

- Richard Carmichael – b. May 1837, bur. 14 Jun 1838 (Burial, **St. Nicholas Without Parish**)

**Richard Carmichael (deceased):**

**Residence - French Street - before June 14, 1838**

**Age at Death - 13 months**

- Richard Carmichael – b. 1779, bur. 16 Jun 1849 (Burial, **St. George Parish**)

**Richard Carmichael (deceased):**

**Residence - North Rutland Square - before June 16, 1849**

**Age at Death - 70 years**

- Robert Carmichael – bur. 6 Jul 1805 (Burial, **St. Paul Parish**)

- Roger Carmichael – bur. 23 Nov 1759 (Burial, **St. Paul Parish**)

# Carmichael Surname Ireland: 1600s to 1900s

- Thomas Carmichael – bur. 14 Mar 1792 (Burial, **St. Peter Parish**)

**Thomas Carmichael (deceased):**

    Residence - Camden Street - before March 14, 1792

    Place of Burial - St. Kevin's Cemetery

- Thomas Carmichael – b. 29 Jan 1833, bur. 31 Jan 1833 (Burial, **St. Peter Parish**)

**Thomas Carmichael (deceased):**

    Residence - Camden Street - before January 31, 1833

    Age at Death - 3 days

    Place of Burial - St. Peter's Cemetery

- Unknown Carmichael – bur. 11 Sep 1778 (Burial, **St. Nicholas Without Parish**)

**Unknown Carmichael (deceased):**

    Residence - Wood Street - before September 11, 1778

- Unknown Carmichael – bur. 16 Nov 1780 (Burial, **St. Nicholas Without Parish**)

**Unknown Carmichael (deceased):**

    Residence - Bull Alley - before November 16, 1780

- Unknown Carmichael – bur. 18 May 1786 (Burial, **St. Nicholas Without Parish**)
- Unknown Carmichael – bur. 6 Aug 1792 (Burial, **St. Nicholas Without Parish**)

**Unknown Carmichael (deceased):**

    Residence - Coombe - before August 6, 1792

# Hurst

- Unknown Carmichael – bur. 16 Mar 1794 (Burial, **St. Nicholas Without Parish**)

**Unknown Carmichael (deceased):**

    **Residence - Bride's Alley - before March 16, 1794**

- Unknown Carmichael – bur. 26 Apr 1797 (Burial, **St. Nicholas Without Parish**)

- Unknown Carmichael (Child) – bur. 16 Jun 1769 (Burial, **St. Mary Parish**)

**Unknown Carmichael (Child) (deceased):**

    **Residence - Britain Street - before June 16, 1769**

- Unknown Carmichael (Child) – bur. 5 Feb 1796 (Burial, **St. Luke Parish**)

**Unknown Carmichael (Child) (deceased):**

    **Residence - Coombe - before February 5, 1796**

- Unknown Carmichael (Mr.) – bur. 16 Sep 1799 (Burial, **St. Luke Parish**)

**Unknown Carmichael (Mr.) (deceased):**

    **Residence - Braithwaite Street - before September 16, 1799**

- Unknown Carmichael (Mrs.) – bur. 21 Nov 1777 (Burial, **St. Mary Parish**)

**Unknown Carmichael (Mrs.) (deceased):**

    **Residence - Capel Street - before November 21, 1777**

- Walter Carmichael – bur. 18 Aug 1723 (Burial, **St. Catherine Parish**)

**Walter Carmichael (deceased):**

    **Relationship Status at Death - single man**

# Carmichael Surname Ireland: 1600s to 1900s

- William Carmichael – bur. 22 Oct 1755 (Burial, **St. Luke Parish**)

- William Carmichael – b. 1774, bur. 6 Oct 1825 (Burial, **St. George Parish**)

**William Carmichael (deceased):**

   **Age at Death - 51 years**

- William Carmichael – b. 1772, bur. 26 Sep 1826 (Burial, **St. Catherine Parish**)

**William Carmichael (deceased):**

   **Residence - Cheater's Court - before September 26, 1826**

   **Age at Death - 54 years**

- William Carmichael – b. 1816, bur. 25 Jun 1839 (Burial, **St. Nicholas Without Parish**)

**William Carmichael (deceased):**

   **Residence - Stephen's Green - before June 25, 1839**

   **Age at Death - 23 years**

# Individual Marriages

- Anne Mary Carmichael & William Paine – 1 Feb 1838 (Marriage, **St. Peter Parish**)

Anne Mary Carmichael (wife):

   Residence - French Street - February 1, 1838

   Occupation - Spinster - February 1, 1838

William Paine (husband):

   Residence - Francis Street, St. Nicholas Without Parish - February 1, 1838

Wedding Witnesses:

Angl Carmichael & Thomas Gravers

- Bridget Carmichael & Patrick Carroll

   o   Patrick Carroll – b. 6 Jun 1856, bapt. 16 Jun 1856 (Baptism, **St. Nicholas Parish** (RC))

Patrick Carroll (father):

   Residence - 12 Francis Street - June 16, 1856

- Catherine Carmichael & Cornelius (C o r n e l i u s) Quinn

   o   Catherine Quinn – bapt. 18 Dec 1851 (Baptism, **St. Catherine Parish** (RC))

- Eleanor Carmichael & James Stanton

   o   Elizabeth Stanton – bapt. 21 Aug 1781 (Baptism, **St. Nicholas Parish** (RC))

# Carmichael Surname Ireland: 1600s to 1900s

- Eleanor Carmichael & Walter Bourne (B o u r n e) – 1 Jan 1792 (Marriage, **St. Bride Parish**)

**Walter Bourne (husband):**

    Occupation - Esquire - January 1, 1792

- Elizabeth Carmichael & Christopher Graham – 10 Dec 1844 (Marriage, **St. George Parish**)

**Signatures:**

**Elizabeth Carmichael (wife):**

    Residence - St. George Parish - December 10, 1844

**Christopher Graham (husband):**

    Residence - St. George Parish - December 10, 1844

**Wedding Witnesses:**

**Peter T. Dillon & Jane Dillon**

**Signatures:**

# Hurst

- Elizabeth Carmichael & George Shields – 18 Dec 1761 (Marriage, **St. Michan Parish**)

**George Shields (husband):**

    **Occupation - Merchant - December 18, 1761**

- Elizabeth Carmichael & James Byrne (B y r n e) – 30 Nov 1833 (Marriage, **St. Andrew Parish (RC)**)

**Wedding Witnesses:**

**Edward Carmichael & Anne O'Shaughnessy**

- Elizabeth Carmichael & John Campion – 5 Feb 1833 (Marriage, **St. Catherine Parish (RC)**)
- Jane Carmichael & George Gibbs – 22 Dec 1798 (Marriage, **St. Bride Parish**)

**George Gibbs (husband):**

    **Residence - Coole Lodge, Co. Westmeath - December 22, 1798**

    **Occupation - Esquire - December 22, 1798**

- Jane Carmichael & Saumareze Dubourdeau – 1 Aug 1822 (Marriage, **St. Peter Parish**)

**Saumareze Dubourdeau (husband):**

    **Residence -Lisburn - August 1, 1822**

**Wedding Witnesse:**

**Hugh Richard Carmichael**

# Carmichael Surname Ireland: 1600s to 1900s

- Joan Carmichael & Nicholas Hogarty – 5 May 1797 (Marriage, **St. Michan Parish (RC)**)

- Margaret Carmichael & Andrew Buchanan – 4 Aug 1764 (Marriage, **St. Michan Parish**)

**Andrew Buchanan (husband):**

**Occupation - Esquire - August 4, 1764**

- Margaret Carmichael & John O'Flynn

  o Robert O'Flynn – bapt. Dec 1849 (Baptism, **St. Catherine Parish (RC)**)

  o Mary O'Flynn – bapt. 17 May 1852 (Baptism, **St. James Parish (RC)**)

  o Anne Margaret O'Flynn – bapt. 30 Mar 1854 (Baptism, **St. James Parish (RC)**)

**John O'Flynn (father):**

**Residence - Dolphin's Barn - March 30, 1854**

- Margaret Carmichael & Michael Brady

  o Margaret Brady – bapt. 30 Jul 1824 (Baptism, **St. Nicholas Parish (RC)**)

- Margaret Carmichael & Robert McKay

  o Wallace McKay & Esther Kerrigan – 15 May 1898 (Marriage, **St. Mary, Pro Cathedral Parish (RC)**)

**Wallace McKay (son):**

**Residence - 94 Lower Gardiner Street - May 15, 1898**

**Esther Kerrigan, daughter of Patrick Kerrigan & Mary Carroll (daughter-in-law):**

**Residence - 4 Beresford Place - May 15, 1898**

# Hurst

**Wedding Witnesses:**

**Joseph Weir & Frances Carroll**

- Margaret Carmichael & Thomas Wilson – 25 Oct 1789 (Marriage, **St. Bride Parish**)

**Thoms Wilson (husband):**

    *Occupation - Attorney - October 25, 1789*

- Martha Carmichael & James White – 27 Feb 1777 (Marriage, **St. Nicholas Without Parish**)

**Martha Carmichael (wife):**

    *Occupation - Spinster - February 27, 1777*

- Mary Carmichael & George Le Grange – 26 Dec 1794 (Marriage, **St. Peter Parish**)
- Mary Carmichael & Gulielmo Keogh
    - Gulielmo Francis Keogh – b. 1 Sep 1873, bapt. 8 Sep 1873 (Baptism, **St. Agatha Parish** (RC))

**Gulielmo Keogh (father):**

    *Residence - 8 Charlemont Parade - September 8, 1873*

- Mary Carmichael & James Forbes – 13 Oct 1760 (Marriage, **St. Michan Parish**)

**James Forbes (husband):**

    *Occupation - Merchant - October 13, 1760*

# Carmichael Surname Ireland: 1600s to 1900s

- Mary Carmichael & Richard Donnelly – 11 Feb 1835 (Marriage, **St. Andrew Parish** (RC))

- Mary Anne Carmichael & Patrick Fitzharris – 19 Aug 1839 (Marriage, **St. Andrew Parish** (RC))

  o Mary Anne Agnes Fitzharris – bapt. 1840 (Baptism, **St. Andrew Parish** (RC))

  o John Fitzharris – bapt. 1842 (Baptism, **St. Andrew Parish** (RC))

  o Catherine Fitzharris – bapt. 1844 (Baptism, **St. Andrew Parish** (RC))

  o Mary Anne Fitzharris – b. 1849, bapt. 1849 (Baptism, **St. Andrew Parish** (RC))

  o Bridget Fitzharris – b. 1850, bapt. 1850 (Baptism, **St. Andrew Parish** (RC))

  o Teresa Fitzharris – bapt. 1854 (Baptism, **St. Andrew Parish** (RC))

  o Monica Fitzharris – b. 1858, bapt. 1858 (Baptism, **St. Andrew Parish** (RC))

  o William Fitzharris – b. 1860, bapt. 1860 (Baptism, **St. Andrew Parish** (RC))

  o Ellen Fitzharris – b. 1862, bapt. 1862 (Baptism, **St. Andrew Parish** (RC))

**Patrick Fitzharris (father):**

**Residence - 1 Fitzwilliam Lane - 1858**

**Fitzwilliam Lane - 1860**

**4 Lad Lane - 1862**

- Roseanne Carmichael & Michael Davis – 19 May 1844 (Marriage, **St. Andrew Parish** (RC))

  o Christopher Davis – b. 1851, bapt. 1851 (Baptism, **St. Andrew Parish** (RC))

  o Patrick Davis – bapt. 1854 (Baptism, **St. Andrew Parish** (RC))

  o Caroline Davis – b. 1859, bapt. 1859 (Baptism, **St. Andrew Parish** (RC))

  o Mary Davis – b. 1861, bapt. 1861 (Baptism, **St. Andrew Parish** (RC))

  o Elizabeth Davis & Bartholomew Doyle – 30 May 1880 (Marriage, **Rathmines Parish** (RC))

# Hurst

Elizabeth Davis (daughter):

Residence - Charlemont Place - May 30, 1880

Bartholomew Doyle, son of John Doyle & Elizabeth Russell (son-in-law):

Residence - Irish Town - May 30, 1880

Michael Davis (father):

Residence - 1 Leeson Lane - 1859

15 Cuffe Street - 1861

- Sarah Carmichael & Bartholomew Cooke – 10 Jul 1779 (Marriage, St. Anne Parish)
- Sarah Elizabeth Carmichael & William Oldham – 14 Apr 1835 (Marriage, St. Peter Parish)

Sarah Elizabeth Carmichael (wife):

Residence - French Street - April 14, 1835

Occupation - Spinster - April 14, 1835

William Oldham (husband):

Residence - 7 French Street - April 14, 1835

Wedding Witnesses:

James Carmichael & Thomas Pickering

# Carmichael Surname Ireland: 1600s to 1900s

- Susan Carmichael & James Byrne (B y r n e)

  o Mary Byrne (B y r n e) & Patrick O'Callaghan – 9 Jan 1865 (Marriage, **Rathmines Parish (RC)**)

**Mary Byrne (daughter):**

    Residence - Ranelagh - January 9, 1865

**Patrick O'Callaghan, son of Patrick O'Callaghan & Catherine McCarthy (son-in-law):**

    Residence - Charlemont Street - January 9, 1865

- Susan Carmichael & Thomas Wilkinson – 23 Apr 1724 (Marriage, **St. Michael Parish**)

# Name Variations

Includes Latin and Abbreviated forms of names found in the original documents.

Abigail = Abigale, Abigall

Anne = Ann, Anna, Annae

Bartholomew = Barth, Bartholmeus, Bartholomeo

Bridget = Birgis, Brigid, Brigida, Bridgit

Catherine = Catharine, Catharina, Catharinae, Catherina, Cath, Catha, Cathae, Cathe, Cathn, Kate

Charles = Carolus, Charls, Chas

Christopher = Christoph

Daniel = Danielem, Danielis

Edmund = Edmond

Edward = Ed, Edwd

Eleanor = Eleo, Eleonora, Elinor, Ellenor

Elizabeth = Betty, Elisa, Elisabeth, Eliz, Eliza, Elizab, Elizh, Elizth

Ellen = Elena, Ellena

Emily = Emilia

Esther = Essie, Ester

Francis = Fransicum

George = Geo, Georg, Georgius

Grace = Gratiae

Gulielmo = Guil, Guillelmi, Gulielmum, Guillelmus, Gulmi

Helen = Helena

# Carmichael Surname Ireland: 1600s to 1900s

**Honor** = Hanora, Honora

**James** = Jacobi, Jacobus, Jas

**Jane** = Joanna

**Jeanne** = Jeannae, Joannae

**Joan** = Johanna, Joney

**John** = Jno, Joannem, Joannes, Johannis

**Joseph** = Jos

**Juliana** = Julian

**Leticia** = Letitia, Lettice, Letticia

**Lewis** = Louis

**Luke** = Lucas

**Margaret** = Margarita, Margaritae, Margeret, Marget, Margt

**Martha** = Marthae

**Mary** = Maria, My

**Mary Anne** = Marianna, Marianne, Maryanne

**Michael** = Michaelis, Michl

**Patrick** = Pat, Patt, Patk, Patricii, Patricius

**Peter** = Petri

**Richard** = Ricardi, Ricardus, Rich, Richd

**Robert** = Roberti

**Rose** = Rosa, Rosae

**Thomas** = Thom, Thomae, Thoms, Thos, Ths

**Timothy** = Timotheus, Timy

**William** = Wil, Will, Willm, Wm

# Notes

# Notes

# Notes

# Notes

# Notes

# Notes

# Index

# Hurst

# Carmichael Surname Ireland: 1600s to 1900s

# Hurst

# Carmichael Surname Ireland: 1600s to 1900s

## T

## U

## W

# About The Author

Donovan Hurst graduated from San Diego State University with a Bachelor of Arts in the major field of studies of History and a minor in the field of studies of Anthropology. He is a current member of The General Society of Mayflower Descendants and has been conducting genealogical research for over 10 years tracing back his ancestors to their ancestral homelands in Denmark, England, France, Germany, Ireland, Norway, and Scotland.

www.ingramcontent.com/pod-product-compliance
Lightning Source LLC
Chambersburg PA
CBHW081158270326
41930CB00014B/3204